know your
MONKEY

Published by ECW PRESS
2120 Queen Street East, Suite 200, Toronto, Ontario, Canada M4E 1E2

NATIONAL LIBRARY OF CANADA CATALOGUING IN PUBLICATION

Friedman, Elyse, 1963–
Know your monkey / Elyse Friedman.
Poems
ISBN 1-55022-613-4

1. Title.

PS8561.R4924K56 2003   C811'.54   C2003-902191-2
PR9199.3.F757K56 2003

Editor: Michael Holmes
Cover and Text Design: Alex Ross
Production & Typesetting: Mary Bowness
Printing: Marc Veilleux

This book is set in Avenir and Bembo

The publication of *Know Your Monkey* has been generously
supported by the Canada Council, the Ontario Arts Council, the Ontario
Media Development Corporation, and the Government of Canada through
the Book Publishing Industry Development Program. Canadä

DISTRIBUTION
CANADA: Jaguar Book Group, 100 Armstrong Avenue, Georgetown, ON, L7G 5S4

PRINTED AND BOUND IN CANADA

ECW PRESS
ecwpress.com

know your
MONKEY

elyse friedman

MISFIT

ecw press

Table of Contents

For Randall Cole

19 Minutes Until You

Studies show
that men think
about sex
every 7 minutes

I think
about these studies
every 4 minutes

Every 16 minutes
I think about cancer

Every 12 minutes
cigarette

Poverty: 40
Success: 42
Laundry: 780
Weight gain: 11

A terrorist attack
every 218 minutes

Every 10,080
I think about that moth
the kind with owl eye
markings on its wings
to scare off predators,
and how that's as close
as you can get to
proof of
God

Paradise Mural

When I was 13-years-old
I worked at the Yorkdale Holiday Inn
selling liquor tickets
at the Thursday night singles' dance

My dad managed the hotel
and my Uncle Eddy ran the dances
that's how I got the job

In between numbers
or sometimes during
the men and women
would come
sweaty
out of the ballroom
to buy their tickets
and get their drinks

The men liked to
kid around
and tipped well
The women disliked having a
kid around
and didn't tip at all

They would eye
my young flesh
the men
and offer to buy me
Cokes
which I got for free
anyways, thanks

And the band would play
the same songs
week after week
the same singles
After The Lovin'
Twilight Time
You Are So Beautiful To Me

And the whole thing seemed
pretty miserable
especially
the lady in the halter gown
with the miles of blue ribbon
woven in her hair
like some kind of Easter basket
mounted on top of her head

And the one who always tried to giggle
but it came off the gangplank of her tongue
like it had been
pushed

And my Uncle Eddy in his captain's hat
and his pinky ring
and his much too Old Spice
and those terrible sad eyes
that didn't change when he smiled
chatting them all up
flattering
buying drinks
for the ladies
and just
trying

to keep it going
make a bit of coin
and maybe
maybe
take one home
for the night
to that crazy apartment
with the view of the ocean
the glorious beach
the magnificent sunset
and the wrinkled palm trees
around the edges
where the wallpaper
didn't get smoothed down
properly

Now He Hosts a Show on CBC

We were drunk
in front of fire
when Jeff decided to
never write
real estate
copy again

He slid giddy across hardwood
into bedroom /office
returned flushed and fevered
with the monster portfolio

Then into the flames
with a *hardy har har* went
the coffered ceilings
features & finishes
Corinthian columns &
commitments to quality

When the cubicle hours of ads
had been torched
he peeled off socks
and burned those too

Focus

Focus
she said
that's what it's about

If you had only focused
on something
you would be
somewhere
by now

Most people
by now
are somewhere

She tore the top off her muffin

I mean, it's fine to try things
but you have to pick something

Pick something
and focus

I watched her chew

Choo-choo

Train. Hobo. Bandana. Halloween.
Candy Apple. Razor Blade. Headline. Shock.

Are you listening? she said

O yes, I said,
turning inside out under water
flashing guilty on my laundry
thinking of cancer
daffodils
that unfortunate link
the absurdly exposed midriff of the waitress
the sore in my cheek from a thousand Nicorettes
the need for a better delivery system
a beverage stronger than coffee
the impossibility of cheerful
the fact that I have nothing to complain about

I watched a gray dog sniff a cement post
Dirty fly on window between

I was hopping blind (a tense tightrope)
Running hard (a blue city)

Running fast

Getting nowhere

Not focused

Hospital Scene

don't remember me
this way
she said
but the years of
warm and good
-come apart
like ice in
spring river
while
bedsores
and bile
dark green in silver
receptacle
slosh hot
in the brain
first
the hair goes
then
the flesh
collapses
finally
a blue-veined
hand
grabs
my wrist
hard
with sudden
ferocious strength
she says:
i want this to stop

and of course
it does

The Great Thing My Cousin George Did

the man said
he would give him
and a friend
fifty bucks each
to drive the
two cars
to hamilton
by six o'clock
that day

my cousin
said OK

then pocketed
the extra fifty
and drove the
two cars
himself

100 yards
then hop out
run back to
the other
car
100 yards past the first
car

hop out
run back to
the other
car

and so on

and so on
with the polio
leg
all the way
to hamilton

twelve hours

he ran
on the shoulder
of the QEW

feeling cocky
wild
and
unspeakably rich
with a whole hundred
big ones
filling the
skinny pocket
of his raggedy
jeans

Screenwriting 101

In movies
characters must always have an
arc.
If the protagonist starts out timid
he must, within the course of 120 minutes,
become BOLD.
If on page one, Little Miss Muffet
sits on her tuffet
she must, by the 95th page,
have left that low seat,
battled fiercely and repeatedly
the spider,
and returned to her perch
triumphant & self-actualized,
without the need for whey.

The antagonist, too, is expected
to change.
Ditto the supporting characters.

Where's the arc? say the story editors.
More arc! More arc! cry the producers.

Of course, in life nobody changes
within the course of 120 minutes.
And very few within the course
of 120 days or months.

Followers don't instantly become
leaders.
The meek rarely make it to
mighty.

The intractable don't melt into
malleability.
The malcontents aren't easily
mollified.

In life, cheaters do prosper, and rarely
become models of virtue.

The beleaguered don't fight
the good fight.
The greedy seldom
give it away.
You won't find the philanderer
high-tailing it home.

The depressives don't dance
happy through the days.
And you can forget about the obsessive
just forgetting about it.

The jealous won't call off
the private dicks.
The sly aren't suddenly on
the up and up.
The coward won't
muster his courage.

The lazy will not turn over
a new leaf
or any leaf.
The aggressive keep swinging
and swinging.

120 minutes will not lead to change.
120 therapy sessions won't either.

At one time a movie
could mirror a life.
The audience could learn
even if the main character didn't.
But that's over.
Now each celluloid journey follows
the same dreary map.
The travelers may appear
in different guises
but they all arrive
at the same destination
at the same time.

It's a foregone conclusion.
An arc.

Adaptation

A middle-aged woman
is flying over Toronto
on a lawn chair

She is not beautiful
She has no super powers
It would not make a good movie

The woman has had a rough day
& this floating thing
is going to help her relax

She is clutching tight the shiny
vinyl bands stretched
taut over aluminum

She hopes there will be no snapping
tipping or slamming into things
like billboards, for example, or seagulls

Life has been loud as of late
Tiny wars raging
& chaos more than a theory

She wants less drama
less action
fewer turning points

She wants more sleep
of the deep
& restful type

She wants coffee & newspaper some

hours at the keyboard & no producers
calling to committee comment on output

Heart attack did not kill
Douglas Adams
Screenwriting did

Poem

No moon
No June
No prairie sky
No orchid
No rose
No gently curving spine
No lips
No eyes
No call of the loon
No grandmother's hands
No storm tossed sea

Just a fart
so loud
it woke us up
Much guffaw
before we
both
fell back asleep

Bleeding & Laughing at Pineway & Cummer

I fell out
of the back of
a van once

wearing high heels
and an evening gown

Grade nine prom
don't you know

Color My World
and Bohemian Rhapsody
didn't do it for us

It was
airplane bottles of vodka
and Colombian flower tops
behind the school
by the tracks

Then into Hinkley's
rust bucket love nest
with my grass-stained
royal blue
velveteen number
and Melanie and Steve and
John Bean and Paul Ryder
We tore through
the suburbs
with radio blaring
Max Webster
Black Sabbath
Led Zeppelin

Deep Purple
teetering high
on my spikes
off balance
and howling
dizzy with spring
and spirits and speed
and Ryder's rough
arms circling around
my blue waist
Then Hinkley hits brakes
too hard
for a cat
and we pitch forward
across metal into seats
and someone screams
Christ! What the fuck are ya doin'?
then
Hinkley hits gas
and four fly backwards
spill onto concrete
stunned
and tangled
and a porch light
comes on
and I can hear crickets
a father steps out
says
Marion, call an ambulance
and the stars are shining
three dogs are barking
the lawns smell good
I am bleeding and laughing

The Writer

There he is
washing socks
in the basement
of that building
across the street

See him
in low light
doing laundry
& writing in a book

Even from this distance
he is ugly

Hunch ugly

But less so
when he writes in the book

What could it be?
Letter to friend?

I'm fine
How are you?
How is Michigan?

Or something better?

I admit I have
imbued him with
powers mystical
& large

No doubt
the words are
singeing the page
singeing the page
as the Stanfield's tumble
and the towels twirl

Magic, manic, miracle words
that would make
daisies scream
snowflakes bleed
fish leave the ocean

Words that would
puncture tires
ignite fires
cause teeth to spontaneously whiten

Words to cure
colds uncommon
make bells sing
and bats ring

Words that
harden cocks
and lift skirts

Fog windows
and wash them too

Words that
dance
like human step dervish
La la la
on funny acid

Words like
pearls in
stinking oysters

Immortal & gravity defying

Crossing against the light
or pyramid balancing
in cold lake
on pink water ski
in new July

Words that settle debts
erase regrets
feed the hungry

Pashmina words
Henkel sharp
that warm the blood
and cool the cranium

Words of steel
that scrape
sky

Burst open
like tulip
in purple time lapse

There he is
in a low light

Should I cross the street?

No

Folklorama

The auditorium
is warm tonight
Portugal has arrived
in Winnipeg
Capable women
doughy-armed whisk
by with trays
of food

Little kids
run madly
with cousins
around uncles
aunts
and long tables
crammed with
tourists

The entertainer
has pants
too tight
he sings
with a Tom Jones
thrust
and the
lip-glossed girls
swoon
for his Mediterranean
beauty

As the band plays
and the men drink
the hard edges of

the gymnasium fade

The grayness goes
and suddenly there is heat
and light
in Winnipeg

Blame It on Asthma

being sick
when you're a kid
gives you
perspective

you see how
the world moves
happily along
without you
and how that
old, other world
is really just one
tiny beehive
of busyness

you get used to
sitting still
while others
race around

you lie quietly
in parks and gardens
while they lurch madly
through offices and subways

you sample the warm perfect
of afternoon naps
growing sleepy
as you watch
the dust float
through a triangle
of sun

or an old
black & white movie
on TV

these good parts
you don't forget

and eventually
you end up jobless

or freelance

Sorry, Robyn

My sister asked me to water her plants while she
    was in Mexico
I agreed, anxious to have access to her apartment
    without her around
I enjoyed going through her things
opening drawers, trying on clothes
looking through kitchen cupboards and eating
a cracker here, a handful of trail mix there
I liked lying on the couch
using the converter to change channels on the
    big-screen TV
She had a good bathtub, nice and deep
loofahs, gels, soaps
green apple, melon, avocado
There was a device to curl eyelashes
a stack of magazines and
a record collection vast
with CD player and over 400 titles
It was great just to lie in bed and listen to music
the bedspread antique
heavy, smooth and cool to the touch
satin blue and gold
I'd lie there and talk on the high-tech phone
it reached the bed no problem and had speed dial
call waiting and caller I.D.
There were musical instruments too
piano, mandolin, castanets,
and those shaky things for rhythm
I had a wonderful week
but forgot about the plants
They all died
and my sister couldn't see
how that could happen

Affection

Mostly they appall me
Humans
Their scrabbling hunger
Their love me love me
Their I'm going to kill you

But sometimes
it changes
and suddenly
for no reason
the opposite

The acne man pale on the subway
Bleached beehive cashier in Hungarian butcher
The teen girl walking awkward on heels
who regrets having pop-topped in public
The last of the Italian chestnut salesman
red cart outside ROM
scooping cashews into paper bags
hot and salty
tiny white bags
And the knapsack boys
with the falling down jeans
The Zaidy transferring food from mouth
to baby
like a bird

I feel
          tender
I want
          to protect
them

These Days

He's always been afraid
to fly
Now more than ever

A letter arrives from unknown source
He thinks anthrax
He thinks plague

A mosquito bit him
West Nile Virus

Burger for lunch
Mad Cow Disease

Subway / SARS

Sun / Melanoma

Water / E coli

Sex / AIDS

He says cell phones
cause brain tumors

But won't he need one when
he's trapped in the rubble?

Shouldn't he be careful?
Shouldn't he be full of care?

Even email
contains virus
these days

Know Your Monkey

Nat Sherman Cigaretellos.
Nicotine patches.
Nicotine gum.

Coming on meek
then lashing out.

Caffeine.

Thinking I'm cold when
it's warm all around.

Junk Yard Dogs,
the meaner the better.

Phenylethylamine.
Dopamine.
Norepinephrine.

Jumping and
jumping and
never even looking.

Not knowing a good
thing when I've got it.

Forward

My hair smells like smoke

All the bridges ablaze &

Crumpling in my wake

I Was Nineteen

think we slept together
once
(as in sleep, as in slumber)
on his way home
after
post–work
post–dinner
fuck
got him at the door
all dressed and ready
got to him
at the door
hand on crotch
tongue in ear

come back to bed
baby
back to bed
he came
and somehow
drifted off
in my arms
so beaut
to watch
him doze
while
fat flakes settled
drunken bumble bee
in streetlamp light
in bedroom window

in the morning
PANIC

in the morning
RAGE

car buried in
snowbank!

i stood and watched
as he cursed
and shoveled

as he furiously
tried to
dig his way
out

3:21. . .

. . . in the morning
and i'm up without
the dawn or a clue
with
the heart pounding
hard
and the beginning
of a hangover
happening
behind
the left eye

i look out the window
and see my
good blue bike
sitting in the night
smiling in its sleep
waiting
for tomorrow
and me

we'll go to assiniboine park
as usual
or to the end of grosvenor
past the tracks

or over to mark morton's
for some stoop sitting
some mid-afternoon
shit shooting
while everyone else in the world
works
(except those kids who pass by

i liked the one with the patch on one eye
you liked the one with the broken shoe)

Canada's Greatest Living Poet

We're at the Imperial Pub
for a reading
I expect little
and there's even less

One after another
sad babies
get up and drool
precious poetry voices
rising and falling
hells bellows
in velvet
yellow pants
pineapple
nose rings
felt jester
helmets
over
Rubik's cube brains

One exceptionally
irritating waif
with limp rat
moustache
whines about
meagre Can. Council winnings
sends
us snoozing
with too long
mope that
strings together
place names
and not much else

Kuala Lumpur blah blah blah
Kigali, Rwanda
blah blah Guyana...

We wait and hang
like dusty dead
exoskeleton
until
a vision
from the back
of the bar
skunky drunk
twisted gray
and bent
weaves like
ancient marionette
to bewildered reader
and shouts: *The corpse that wouldn't rot!*

Then Canada's greatest living poet
leaves the pub
laughing

Should Have Been Working

rode to the park today
heavy clover
with topnote
of sweat
too sweet
for words, intoxicating
dizzying
fell lazy into
grass
heard bumble bee
buzz
& watched
white forms moving
against green earth

playing cricket
they were

moving against the green
dark
muscled limbs
white trousers & shirts
tugged by breeze
airy & blowing
blazing white
against green

the way they moved
to me made no sense
i watched
without comprehending
the changing of places the
shifting of bodies the

hypnotic ballet of muscled
dark limbs
and fiery whiteness
blazing soft
here and there
against the green

Art Saves Your Ass

it was probably one of the worst
things I ever did
a B & E
we entered
yeah
but we didn't really break
kathy had the key
to her cousin's townhouse
across the way
squeaky clean cousin
into bay city rollers
if i recall correctly
they had gone to the cottage
and we needed a place to party
john, paul and paul
redhead, blond and brunette
i was with the blond
paul reid
strange
i don't care for blonds
anyway
we went in
smoked tons
of pot
drank all their beer
cases and cases
in the basement
tried something that was
supposedly meth
but wasn't
read the kid's diary
and finally
fucked in the parents' room

my second time
only
sixteen years old
the blond
said he loved me
in the wide bed
and held me all
night
what a mess
in the morning
i went
stinking of sex
and smoke
onto this bus
then that one
then the subway
then walked
down
to
harbourfront
where the
innerstage theatre company
was practising
the snow queen
i
was the snow queen
i
did the relaxation exercises
and sang the "face to face with evil" number
while everyone else
john, paul, paul and kathy
got arrested
'cause

of course
the dad
came home
early

Sad & Good

how you will feel
in spring
when you see
the back of
a young man's neck
shaved
with the ears
sticking out
all earnest
handsome
and sturdy

same as
eating
icing sugar pastry
for breakfast
in another country
with the sun
shining down
on cappucino foam
the gurgle of the machine
everything
warm and sweet and
about to be
memory

Life Is Hard

I like the ones that walk along
with mouths full of
scram!
and eyes full of
help!

You see them
middle of the day
shuffling
across streets
in sweaters too warm
for the weather

They used to look
much older
than they do now
much odder
too
but that was just
me
before
not knowing
all about
it

Pastime

I like to go to pool halls
and play foosball
with the young boys
I like to beat them
and I do
(all those afternoons
playing hooky
from Zion Heights
Junior High)

Saunter to the table
and suss the situation
Sucking on a cig
sizing up the scene

Hold two quarters in the air
and say: Anyone want to play?

...I'll pay

They smile and shrug
several step aside
and the youngest
worst player
takes me on
WHAM
I score right away
everybody laughs

Uh oh, Tony, look out
the lady's good
Tony says:
Ahh, that was bullshit, man

WHAM
I sink another
Sharp crack of ball on metal
more laughs
except from Tony

Soon enough
the rookie is gone
and the next best guy —
swig of beer
light a smoke
push up the flannel shirt sleeves —
takes me on

And so on
and so on
until I've moved
through the ranks
and I'm
sweating and rocking
in the rhythm
of the thing

Sometimes
I'll dare them to go
two on one
but sometimes I
just step back and watch

The grim-faced one
with the black t-shirt
and the blue-veined
biceps

The tall one
with the nice moves
and the snarly
lips

The stocky one
with the curly hair
and the cocky
posturing

I think I'm
too old
for this
game

Sad But True

there was plenty of fucking
but very few words
hardly any talk at all
except about work
which made sense
since he was my boss

i would crack jokes
he would laugh
then go about his business
and me about my worshipping
later, we'd meet in terrible restaurants
then off to my place before home to wife

he was remarkably shallow
smart in some ways
stupid in more
but much charisma
i'd never encountered
anything like it

a monstrous light and shake
every time he entered a room
cigar in one hand
drink in the other
each time I heard that voice in the hall
i would pull myself up and prepare

petty, vapid, cruel
and i revered with every drop of blood
every cell
like never before
completely content to be in orbit

around the dark star

once only, genuine bliss
stretched out on a warm island in july
miles from work and city
squinting at the sun and the silhouette of a man
gathering blueberries in a cup
for my lips

Something Like That

he says
i walk
like a pimp
well okay
i'm just about
as low

we watched
together
desdemona
bite it
on a big screen
then immediately
after
drinks
smokes
a subway
ride
home
and my
hand
pressed
hard
against
his
crotch

i walk
like
a pimp

on home
to the other
and he says:
how was
your day?

Maybe It Can Happen Again

old man
gets on
the subway

on his
arm
a number
he folds
carefully
another number
on a ticket
into his wallet

and i think
sir
you already
won
the lottery

Juden

Fired by hate

like clay in kiln

made hard and

easily broken.

Meltdown

The way Polaroids burn
is interesting
I watched your head puff up
like Jiffy-Pop
and burst
smoke spewing
out of your
face
a horrible stink
and you were gone

Now, five months later
I'm enjoying a martini
for breakfast
minus the olive
and vermouth
flaming some other shots
of me
trying to look casual
as if caught off-guard
but in reality
posed
phony
deserving to burn
like you

Check Up

In the waiting room,
trying to choose between
heart and skin disease
pamphlets, when a woman with
a moustache walks in.
Full and furry.
I look quickly away,
select heart disease and sit.
She sits.
I glance as she pulls book from bag
and commences reading.
Shiny paperback: *Sammy Keyes &*
the Curse of Moustache Mary.
I try not to laugh.
I try to comprehend
how a thing such as this can occur.
I stare hard at the diseased heart info.
I read that heart disease pamphlet
seven or eight times.

Drunk Drivers Against Mad Mothers

Dear Friend,
My cousin Brendan was only 26 years old
He was so special, so wonderful.

Brendan was a handful, always on the go.
He loved hockey and "hanging out" with his friends.
There was never a dull moment.

But Brendan's gone. Gord and Mike
and Sally and I will have to spend the rest
of our weekends without this bright light.

Brendan was taken from us. He was taken by a 15-
    year-old
who had been cycling down Main Street on the
    morning
after an all-night house party that Brendan attended.

Brendan was driving a mini-van. He had consumed
    alcohol
and didn't see the boy on the bike. He plowed into
    him. Brendan
escaped without injury, but was placed behind bars.

The Mad Mother who made sure Brendan would stay
locked up for the rest of his life, didn't show any
    remorse,
none at all, for what she did.

I'm not telling you about Brendan
to ask for your sympathy.
I'm writing to ask for something else entirely.

I'm asking you to join me in fighting to keep what
happened to Brendan and to us from happening
to others — maybe even someone in your own
    peer group.

My peer group became involved in DDAMM Canada
    immediately after
Brendan was locked up. In fact, my friend Lucy
    passed out some 900
DDAMM Canada ribbons at Brendan's trial.

If we can prevent even one incarceration
of an impaired driver, perhaps Brendan's
internment will at least have some meaning.

So I'm asking you today to do two things, really.
The first is to join DDAMM Canada and help support
the kinds of programs that can put an end to this
    nightmare.

Second, I ask you, please, to tell one person today
about
DDAMM Canada. Ask that person to tell one other
    person.
If we all do that we can make a difference.

Thank you for reading my letter.

Defending Rebecca

At a cafe on Queen
girl says:
"Sherry's got the dirt on
Rebecca E."
Around the table
lips are licked
in anticipation
"Well," says Sherry
gleeful,
"I used to work at the same bar.
She slept with all band members
who came in. Big bad slut, eh!"

"Yeah right," says I.

Eyebrows raise and point at me.

I know these things, girly.
She was probably
too pretty
for the other bar maidens
to handle,
probably tongued a
drummer once.
Big deal.
And besides —
even true —
who cares?

"So what," says I.
"What she
supposed to do,
hide in her room

and read Judy Blume
like the rest of YOUSE?
I think it's good she got
some carefree fucks in
before AIDS."

Silence.

Disapproval.

Bread sticks
snap like spines
and I'm on
the outside
again.

Prematurely Gray

She stands in the bathroom
staring at herself in the mirror
for twenty, thirty minutes at a time
staring at her skin
"I don't recognize myself anymore,"
she says when he comes in
to piss
He shakes off
leaves
he's heard it before

Sometimes she takes
the hand mirror to the window
stares at herself in the
bright noon light
horrified
and
fascinated
by this new
surface
this line
that bump
or hollow

He finds
the mirror lying
by different
panes around the house

In the morning
she catches herself
in the kettle
the big black

circles
filling the kitchen as she
leans in for a better look
and even before
she's had her coffee
she thinks about
death
and gin

The Always Illicit Blue Boy

I remember the
phone calls.
Breathing.
Listening.
Hello? Hello...?
I knew
it was you.
And poems scrawled
on coasters, sent over
in taxis.
Flowers that ended
up at my sister's.
You came
in my hand
on the roof of the
Park Plaza.
Remember?
Nice view.

And eighteen years before when
the bodies were perfect,
built
for lust
in daytime apartments.
I showed up at your party.
A clique breach.
A dust up.
The 'freak' infiltrating
the 'gym bag gang.'
"Don't go," you said, circling my wrist
with your hand.
Bye bye.
But you knew

I'd be back.

A Maritime sweater.
A Stan Rogers cassette.
A Player's Extra Light
between chapped lips.
You made fettuccine Alfredo
with a hair in it.
I fell asleep in your bathtub.
We missed the important
Student Awards night.
You made me a sandwich.
Said "How is it?"
"Good," I said.
"'Cause the cheese is kind of old."
I looked inside. Curled and cracked.
The George Burns of fromage.
And you let me cut your hair.
You believed I could do that.
I love that you believed.
And when I turned you into Moe
from the Three Stooges
you did not get angry.
Not even mock eye poke.
And you helped
make my movie.
All night A & B
rolling in room BB10.

I think you wanted
the guard to walk
in on us.

Was It the Leather Jacket?

Went to the bank to pick up
some money
that had been wired to me
and even though
I asked for it
and knew the amount
who it was from
who it was for
the cashier
was suspicious
surveying me
with her stupid
eyes
and her frosted tips
and her ugly sweater

I laid my I.D. on the counter
credit card and bank card
   Driver's licence? she said
I laid that down too
    Social insurance card? she asked
No
   Birth certificate?
No
    Well, usually we need two pieces of I.D.
Well, you have three pieces, do you not?

Lips tightened as she waddled
off to find a signature
someone else
to take
the blame

How much did you say your husband was
sending?
Stony face
Oh sorry, is it your father? I didn't mean
to assume . . .
My pimp, actually
is what I wanted to say
but I knew that
that wouldn't
get me the money
any faster

Signs

if i should smoke
leap into that tree

if i shouldn't smoke
leap into that tree

but the squirrel
doesn't budge
and i'm going to
have to decide

I Love

You
went to Montreal
and I saw your shoes
in the hall
Reeboks curled
in the shape of your feet
in the odd way you walk
and I realized
how much
how much
how much

Locked Out

this apartment
gets worse
all the time
today
went down
to do laundry
wet clothes in dryer
then *uh oh*
no change and
shit
no keys
rang the super
didn't answer
passed out drunk
or cowering
in bedroom
overflowing toilet . . . backed up sink . . . kitchen fire . . .
i understand
but still
i'm standing
with wet sweaters
you know?
thought I'd use a phone
call boyfriend or sister
knocked on many doors
no one opened
heard TVs in background, lapdogs barking
saw scared
old eyes
covering peep holes
chicken eyes
wondering why and what and what?

the wig lady didn't let me in
the cane lady didn't let me in
the shopping cart lady didn't let me in

the old man who is always outside
walking
smiling
eating oranges in the park
would have let me in
but he was outside
walking, smiling, etc.

still
fogies
make the best neighbours
don't play music
can't hear mine
not always moving
in and out
leaving
futons smelly
on the curb
hardly ever
do laundry
or make conversation

if i move
i'll go to retirement villa
but i'll make
extra keys

A Tender and Affectionate Portrait of Myself

I am middle-aged and afraid. Nails bitten and bleeding. I should lose eleven pounds and get a haircut. My favourite movie is *Harold & Maude*. Occasionally, I'll buy an *Outreach* from the alcoholic homeless person who stands silent outside the liquor store, but never from the fat folksy guy who sits in front of Shoppers Drug Mart and chats with passersby and pats their golden retrievers. I have the following quote taped to my computer keyboard: "In 20 years of psychoanalytic practice I have seen a great deal of neurotics. The most depressed, pitiful and sordid lot has been that of writers." Dr. Edmund Bergler. When I was nine, I sustained a concussion while trying to ice skate down the tobogganing hill. Five years later I went to Italy to lose my virginity. I sleep with a mask on. I dread having to make conversation with my hairdresser. The books nearest to me are: *Ham on Rye, Catcher in the Rye*, and *Anne of Green Gables*. I should exercise more. I have been on the nicotine patch for over five years. It's almost too late to have children. I live alone. I know how to do the Taoist Tai Chi set. Insomnia troubles me. I went to a psychiatrist, but refused to reveal. Felt he was prying. I would have a basset hound, a dachshund and a poodle if I weren't allergic to animals. My boyfriend is six years younger than I am. The basset hound would be called Bruce. I check my email at least twenty times a day. I don't enjoy traveling. I never want to run into my neighbours. I believe that cuisine reveals a lot about a culture. I dislike all cultures equally. The dachshund would be called Irene. When I go to a movie I have to sit on the aisle. I think I have a brain tumor. I require nine hours of sleep per night. I went to an empty beach in Hawaii when it was raining; I body surfed the waves with some Hawaiian kids who kept throwing themselves into my arms and laughing. I sometimes think about that when I'm stressed out, which is most of the time. I like to go to open houses and look at other people's interiors. I like to paint. I want to believe in absolutes. I wish I could make myself invisible. The poodle would be called Richard. I am genuinely surprised when I don't win the lottery. I wish I had a fireplace and a claw foot tub. I wish Steve Goodman were still alive. I think I have lung or throat cancer. I am inordinately fond of Southern accents. I dropped out of school when I was fifteen. I would like to know what happened to David Jafine, JoyAnne Serota and Gord McWilliams. Also Monsieur xx, the French teacher who smoked me up by the railroad tracks behind the junior high and told me to go see *A Clockwork Orange*. I fear exclusion. I fantasize about having dinner in Paris with David Sedaris and his boyfriend. I have a small and meaningless crush on an actor born in 1978. My ex recently got married. I walked away from a thirteen-year relationship. I talk in my sleep. I can beat you at Scrabble and ping-pong. I'm afraid to drive on the highway. Most of my friends are men. I live in Toronto. A lot of my friends live in Winnipeg. I want to go to Newfoundland and the Turks & Caicos, but won't. I will never forgive myself for beating my mother at Scrabble when she had lymphoma. My mother died when I was twenty-two. I think I have lymphoma. I used to write comedy for the radio. I have written two novels, one book of poems and seven movies. If I have a meeting at eleven, I'll wake up at seven thinking I've missed it. I might not sleep at all. I swallow two or three chocolate bars a day. I love the notes of Vic Chesnutt. I carry antibacterial lotion at all times. I eat sleeping pills. I am compulsively punctual. All my possessions can be packed into 50 cardboard cartons. I complain constantly. I am never satisfied. I don't care how much money my boyfriend earns. I have the ability to select winning roulette numbers when I have PMS. I think "Silver Wheels" by Bruce Cockburn is the best driving song. If you put on Klezmer music I will dance around. I believe in magic. I eat dinner in front of the television. On Christmas, I watched five episodes of *Trading Spaces*. "Sad Eyed Lady of The Lowlands" is my favourite song. It's only January and I'm already looking forward to the Academy Awards. When Charles Bukowski died, I went to the race-track and won a triactor in his honour. I don't believe that the poor are noble. I think Doris Day was a great comedienne. *The Apartment* is one of my favourite films. Also *The Inlaws* with Peter Falk and Alan Arkin. Also *Lover Come Back*, which was written by Stanley Shapiro. My boyfriend doesn't want to live with me. I can stare at a fire for hours. I love the smell of smoke. I think he'll eventually leave me for someone younger/more symmetrical. When that happens I will believe her to be less witty, less kind, and more demanding. She will, of course, be stupid. I order groceries online. *Grey Gardens* is my favourite documentary. I'm afraid of Little Edie. I am Little Edie. I wish I had my own washer and dryer. I wish everyone were still alive.

Girlfriend

she invites
me out
for drink
squeals fake
glee over
phone
like some kind
of helium pitched
Joanne Worley
then fizzes
hate
and smiles smug into
her beer
when I come out

why do I come out?

to be bored by this
oily bug
insulted by
this beetle-hearted
hunk of bitter
who would
rather see me
dead/fat/broke/alone

this isn't how it's
supposed to be

yet this is
how it is

Get Those Knees Up

I went to an exercise class this morning
and when it was through
a woman came up to me
and asked if I had Chronic Fatigue Syndrome

Hmm.

Then she started telling me about
her Chronic Fatigue
how she sleeps
on a bed of magnets
and about
her naturopath
her needs dietary
and after only
seven minutes
I knew precisely
how she felt

A Pig Is a Pig

This is Illness,
the likes of which
we have never seen.

Greedy green &
twisted sick
She is core rotten.

A mean fungus oozing
through brain & bowels
(no heart to speak of).

Pincher of pennies.
Torturer of husbands.
Thief / Villain / Devil / Cheat.

A Cancer, a Canker,
the stench of sour wafts
off our Dickensian demon.

Morbid hoarder.
Venal viper.
Bilious blight.

For twenty bucks
she'd rake the guts
from mother or child.

Listen, wolf-girl,
you misery, you miser,
you can't take it with you.

Not even to hell.

Tom, Charles and Me

on a desert island
stranded
the only stuff that
made it:
the typewriter
the drum
a case of napoleon brandy
some cigarettes

hank types
tom sings
i drink coconut milk
and body surf the waves

bukowski lives in sun
spears fish
in wide yellow day
white legs in blue water
the pants rolled high
(i wave from beach. he nods, squinting
in the light. everything sparkles)
tom charms the snake meat
out of the jungle after dark
the bats circle the moon circling
his gently rocking
upturned face

at night
fire
brandy
and laughs

all that good male

all around
me and tom
or buk or both
or sometimes
alone
in my hut
with the distant sound of keys
striking palm leaf
on the one side
and the distant growl
of mad mouth music
on the other

this is everything
i need
this
is
rescue

Too Much

how the heart
can stretch
in ways
that it's not
supposed to

i'm not
supposed to
love
you
& you
& you
but what can
i do
i do

Acknowledgements

Thanks to Alex Ross, Michael Holmes, Mary Bowness, and everyone at ECW PRESS. Thanks to Kevin Connolly for putting in the good word. Warm thanks to Stuart Ross for friendship, support and poetic acuity.